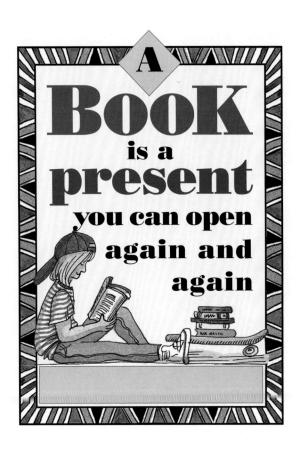

can you find
BIBLE HEROES?

Introducing Your Child to the Old Testament

Written by **Philip D. Gallery**
Illustrated by **Janet L. Harlow**

ST. ANTHONY MESSENGER PRESS
Cincinnati, Ohio

NOVALIS

In praise of the God of Abraham,
Isaac and Jacob

Written by Philip D. Gallery
Illustrated by Janet L. Harlow
Cover and book design by Mary Alfieri and
David A. Juergens/RPI

Copyright ©1998, Philip D. Gallery and Janet L. Harlow

Published in the United States by
St. Anthony Messenger Press
1615 Republic St., Cincinnati, OH 45210-1298

ISBN 0-86716-335-6

Published in Canada by Novalis
49 Front St. E, 2nd Floor,
Toronto, Ontario M5E 1B3 Canada
1-800-387-7164

Canadian Cataloguing-in-Publication Data

Gallery, Philip D.
  Can you find Bible Heroes?: introducing your child to the
Old Testament

ISBN 2-89088-984-X

  1. Heroes in the Bible—Juvenile literature. 2. Bible. O.T.—
Biography—Juvenile literature. 3. Bible stories, English—O.T.
—Juvenile literature. I. Harlow, Janet L. II. Title.

BS539.G35 1998   j221.9'22   C98-900720-0

Printed and bound in the U.S.A. by Worzalla

Contents

Introduction

The Christian Bible contains two Testaments—the Old and the New. But the "Bible" Jesus knew and loved contained only the Hebrew Scriptures—what most Christians call the Old Testament. The way of life revealed by **Can You Find Bible Heroes?** was the Hebrew way of life. Jesus was born and raised Jewish, as were his disciples and most of the early Christians as well. The principles and stories of Judaism guided Jesus as he grew. As a man, Jesus preached to fellow Jews about the Old Testament God of Abraham, Isaac and Jacob. After his death, Jesus' followers wrote the New Testament, under the assumption that those who read it would have some familiarity with the Old Testament. Looking at the New Testament in this light, we begin to see how closely the Old and New Testaments are connected; both are indispensable for Christians.

This book was designed with Jesus' Jewish spiritual upbringing in mind. As a child growing up in a family deeply committed to its Jewish heritage, Jesus was immersed in this culture from an early age. The heroes we have chosen to tell the story of God's relationship with his chosen people are the men and women who were heroes to Jesus and his young friends.

As a child, Jesus was certainly taught the stories of Noah, Abraham, Joseph, Ruth and other Bible heroes by Mary and Joseph. When he was a young man, Jesus probably attended the synagogue school, where he would have studied the first five books of the Bible—the Torah—as well as the Prophets, Psalms and other writings. As a young man, during Sabbath services in the synagogue, Jesus would have heard readings from the Torah and listened to the discussions of those readings carried on by the elders and the teachers.

Just as Jesus needed Mary and Joseph and his teachers to guide him on his spiritual journey, your children need you and the other adults in their lives to guide them. When very young children study the pictures in this book, looking for the Bible heroes hidden in them, the heroes of Jesus' young life will begin to come alive for them. As you help older children read the opening paragraph for each page, and read the Bible verses in the searches, you will be helping to guide them on the spiritual journey taken by Jesus as a young boy. To help on this journey, we have provided, beginning on page 32, a Parent's Guide for each picture. Additionally, the meanings for key words in italics are given in the Glossary on page 39. Finally, each page has a few silly things on it, or things that were not around in Old Testament times. These things are meant to amuse those of you who may be called upon by little voices to go over the book many times.

If these stories, and the heroes who lived them, meant so much to Jesus as a first-century Jewish child, they should mean a great deal to Christian children. As our children learn what Jesus learned, they will come to understand, as Jesus understood, the great prayer of the Jewish people: "Hear, O Israel, the Lord is our God, the Lord is One. Let us praise Him for ever and ever."

Philip Gallery and Janet Harlow

Hidden in Every Picture

These ten things are hidden in every picture. Nine of them are symbols from the Old Testament that would have had special meaning for Jesus as a young Jewish boy. The tenth one is you—and each of us.

Altars were common in the Old Testament (see Search 2: God Saves Noah's Family and the Animals and Search 3: God Calls Abraham to Be the Father of His Chosen People). In Jesus' time, a sheep was sacrificed each day on the altar of the Temple in Jerusalem. This was done to show God that his people wanted to surrender their lives to him, that they were grateful to him and that they were willing to serve him.

Angels are beings created by God to share the joy of heaven. The Jewish people of Jesus' time thought angels were created by God at the beginning of time to serve and praise him. In the Old Testament, angels guarded the entrance to Eden (see Search 1: God Creates the World), spoke to Abraham (see Search 3: God Calls Abraham to Be the Father of His Chosen People), wrestled with Jacob (see Genesis 32:23-31) and served God in many other ways. In the New Testament, angels told Mary she would be the mother of God (see Luke 1:2-38), announced the birth of Jesus (see Luke 2:8-14) and told Joseph to take the baby Jesus into Egypt (see Matthew 2:13-15).

The **apple** represents the fruit that God told Eve and Adam not to eat in the Garden of Eden.

Bread was the most important food for the people of the Old Testament. When God's people needed food on their journey out of Egypt, God gave them bread from the heavens (see Search 5: God Chooses Moses to Lead His People Out of Egypt). Jesus called himself the "bread of life" (see John 6:35) to make it clear that he should be considered the most important reality in a person's life.

Noah sent out a **dove** when he wanted to see if the water from the great flood was going down (see Search 2: God Saves Noah's Family and the Animals). When Jesus was baptized, the Holy Spirit descended on him in the form of a dove (see Luke 3:21-22). Today the dove is considered a sign of peace.

The **lamb** is a special symbol for the Jewish people because it was the blood of lambs that saved the Jewish people from death before they left Egypt (see Search 5: God Chooses Moses to Lead His People Out of Egypt). John the Baptist called Jesus the Lamb of God (see John 1:29) to signify that, by shedding his blood on the cross, Jesus would protect us from the death of the spirit that is caused by sin.

A **rainbow** was the sign from God to Noah that God would never again flood the world (see Search 2: God Saves Noah's Family and the Animals). Because God used a rainbow as a sign of his promise to Noah, many people find in a rainbow the sign of God's special care.

The **shofar** is a ram's horn that the Israelites blew before the walls of Jericho. It was used to pass signals back and forth during battles. It is still blown in synagogues on New Year's Day and the Day of Atonement.

The **Ten Commandments** were written on stone tablets given to Moses by God on Mount Sinai (see Search 5: God Chooses Moses to Lead His People Out of Egypt). God's people carried the tablets with them in the ark of the covenant wherever they went. The Ten Commandments apply to Christians just as much as they apply to Jewish people.

The **child** in modern clothes in each picture shows that the heroes of the Old Testament weren't heroes only for Jesus and his friends but should be heroes for all of us.

SEARCH 1
God Creates the World

In the beginning God was all there was. But God had a lot of love to give, so he decided to *create* people to share his love. But first, he had to create the heavens and the earth. Later, God put you in the world so he could share his *Holy Spirit* of love with you.

God said, "Let there be light," and there was light. After God created the light, he said, "Let the waters under the sky be gathered into one place and let the dry land appear." **CAN YOU FIND THE DRY LAND?**

Then God put two great lights in the sky: one for the day and one for the night. **CAN YOU FIND THE SUN AND THE MOON?**

Finally, God created man and woman in his own *image*. The man was named Adam and the woman was named Eve. **CAN YOU FIND ADAM AND EVE?**

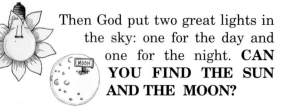

God placed Adam and Eve in the Garden of Eden and gave them everything in the world, but told them not to eat the fruit from the tree of knowledge of good and evil. **CAN YOU FIND THE TREE?**

Adam and Eve did what God told them not to do. They decided to *disobey* God and eat fruit from the tree. So God made them leave the Garden of Eden. Then God put an angel at the gate to the Garden so they couldn't get back in. **CAN YOU FIND THE ANGEL?**

SEARCH 2
God Saves Noah's Family and the Animals

Many years after Adam and Eve were sent from the Garden of Eden, the people of the world were still disobeying God. Because they wouldn't obey him, God was sorry that he had ever made people. One man, however, did obey God. His name was Noah.

Noah was a good man who tried to do what God wanted. **CAN YOU FIND NOAH?**

One day God told Noah to make an *ark* of wood. He told him exactly how to build it and how big it should be. **CAN YOU FIND THE ARK?**

 Next the *Lord* told Noah that he was going to make it rain and bring floodwaters upon the earth. He told Noah and his family to enter the ark and take with them two of every living creature to keep them alive. He also told Noah to take every kind of food on the ark, so his family and the animals could eat. **CAN YOU COUNT THE PAIRS OF ANIMALS?**

It rained for forty days and nights until the land was covered with water. Noah waited a long time for the water to go down. Then he sent a dove out to see if it could find any dry land. When the dove returned with a fresh olive leaf in its beak, Noah knew the water was getting low. **CAN YOU FIND THE DOVE?**

When the ark was back on dry land, Noah built an *altar* to the Lord. Then God made a *covenant* with Noah. God promised never to flood the earth again. As a sign of the covenant, God put a rainbow in the clouds. **CAN YOU FIND THE RAINBOW?**

9

SEARCH 3

God Calls Abraham to Be the Father of his Chosen People

Even after the flood, God saw that people were still having a hard time obeying him. Because he loves us, he made a plan to give us more help. The first thing he did to help us was to pick a person to talk to. The person he picked was named Abraham. God told Abraham to move away from the country he lived in. So Abraham left home with his wife Sarah and his family.

When they arrived in their new home, the Lord promised Abraham he would give this land to his *descendants*. That is why it is called the *promised land*. In thanksgiving to God, Abraham built an altar to the Lord. **CAN YOU FIND THE ALTAR?**

Next, the Lord told Abraham that he would make him the father of many nations. He also promised to *bless* Sarah by giving her a son. **CAN YOU FIND** **ABRAHAM?**

It is very unusual for an old woman to have a baby. Because Sarah was old and had no children, she laughed when she heard God say that she would have a son. **CAN YOU FIND THE LAUGHING SARAH?**

God's promise came true. After their son Isaac was born, God told Abraham to make a *sacrifice* of Isaac. Abraham loved Isaac and did not want anything bad to happen to him, but he was ready to obey God. Abraham climbed a mountain with Isaac and started to sacrifice him. **CAN YOU FIND ABRAHAM AND ISAAC?**

Since God loved Isaac, too, he sent an *angel* to stop the sacrifice. Then Abraham saw a ram caught in a bush and offered it to God in the place of Isaac. **CAN YOU FIND THE RAM?**

SEARCH 4
God Leads Joseph and the Children of Israel Into Egypt

When Isaac grew up, he had a son named Jacob. When Jacob grew up, he had twelve sons. After Jacob's son Joseph was born, God changed Jacob's name to Israel. When Joseph was a young man, some of his brothers didn't like him. They made a plan to get rid of him.

Joseph's brothers took off the special coat his father had given him and threw him into a well. Later, they took him out of the well and sold him to traders, who took him to Egypt as a *slave*. **CAN YOU FIND THE SLAVE JOSEPH?**

Joseph ended up in the palace of the *Pharaoh*. One night in a dream Pharaoh saw seven fat cows being eaten by seven thin cows, and seven fat ears of grain being eaten by seven thin ears. Joseph told Pharaoh his dream meant that Egypt would have seven years of good crops, then seven years of poor crops. **CAN YOU FIND PHARAOH?**

Because Joseph was so wise, Pharaoh put him in charge of storing food to be used during the years of poor crops. **CAN YOU FIND THE POWERFUL JOSEPH?**

The land of *Canaan,* where Joseph's brothers lived, also had poor crops. But they did not store up food like the people in Egypt. So their father, Israel, sent ten of Joseph's brothers to Egypt to buy food. When they got there and met Joseph, they didn't know who he was. **CAN YOU FIND JOSEPH'S TEN BROTHERS?**

 Finally, Joseph told his brothers who he was. Then he told them to bring Israel, and all his family, to live in Egypt. The brothers went home and did as Joseph asked. **CAN YOU FIND ISRAEL?**

SEARCH 5

God Chooses Moses to Lead His People Out of Egypt

Before Joseph died, he told the Israelites that one day God would lead them out of Egypt. Many years later God chose a man named Moses to lead them to the land he had promised Abraham. One day God spoke to Moses out of a burning bush.

God told Moses to go with his brother Aaron to see Pharaoh. They told Pharaoh, "The Lord, the God of the Israelites, says: 'Let my people go so that they may *worship* me.'" But Pharaoh refused. Because of this, God sent ten *plagues*, including a plague of frogs and one of *locusts*, to Egypt. **CAN YOU FIND PHARAOH?**

Finally, God sent a plague of death across Egypt. God told the Israelites to mark their houses with lamb's blood so the plague would pass over them. **CAN YOU FIND THE DOORS?**

Finally, Pharaoh let the Israelites go. As they walked toward the land God had promised to give them, the Sea of Reeds parted and they passed on dry land into the desert. **CAN YOU FIND THE DRY LAND?**

Because there was no food in the desert, God gave the Israelites *manna* from heaven to eat. **CAN YOU COUNT THE MANNA?**

Then God called Moses to Mount Sinai to give him the two *tablets* with the *ten commandments*. **CAN YOU FIND THE TWO TABLETS?**

After forty years in the desert, the Israelites came to the promised land of milk and honey. **CAN YOU FIND MOSES?**

SEARCH 6
God Appoints Joshua to Lead the Israelites

Before Moses died, God told him that Joshua was to take his place as the leader of the Israelites. God told Joshua to be *faithful* and brave because he was going to have to bring the Israelites into the land God had promised to give them. Soon after they arrived in this promised land, the Israelites had to fight a battle.

Joshua sent two *spies* ahead of the Israelites into the city of Jericho. **CAN YOU FIND THE TWO SPIES?**

The spies went to the house of a woman named Rahab. Because she helped them by hiding them from the people of Jericho, they told her to hang a red rope out of her window so that when the Israelites entered the city they would know not to harm anyone in that house. **CAN YOU FIND THE RED ROPE?**

Then the Lord said to Joshua, "Have all the soldiers circle the city, marching around it once, with seven *priests* carrying rams' horns." **CAN YOU FIND JOSHUA?**

Early the next morning, Joshua had the seven priests, blowing their horns, march around the city in front of the *Ark of the Lord*. **CAN YOU FIND THE ARK?**

As the horns blew, the Israelites began to shout and as they shouted, the wall around Jericho fell down. **CAN YOU COUNT THE HORNS?**

SEARCH 7

God Picks Judges to Help His Chosen People

After Joshua died, the Israelites struggled to settle in the promised land. They sometimes lost *faith* in God and got into trouble. The men and women God sent to help them were called judges.

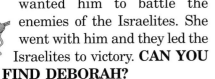

The *prophetess* Deborah, who was judging Israel, told a man named Barak that God wanted him to battle the enemies of the Israelites. She went with him and they led the Israelites to victory. **CAN YOU FIND DEBORAH?**

The Israelites were under the power of the *Midianites*. God told a new judge named Gideon to go to their *camp*. Gideon's men blew horns and waved torches. The Midianites became confused and ran away. **CAN YOU FIND GIDEON?**

God told Samson never to allow his hair to be cut. As long as he obeyed, he was stronger than his enemies. But he was tricked into letting his hair be cut, and the *Philistines* captured him. They tied Samson to the columns of their temple and made fun of him. Samson asked God to strengthen him one last time. He pushed on the columns and the temple fell. **CAN YOU FIND SAMSON?**

Eli had two *evil* sons. He told them to love God. They wouldn't listen, and they were killed and the Ark of the Lord was captured by the Philistines. When Eli heard the news, he died. **CAN YOU FIND ELI?**

Wherever the Philistines took the Ark, plagues followed them, so they decided to give it back. After it was returned, Samuel, who was the new judge, told the Israelites to return to the Lord. **CAN YOU FIND SAMUEL?**

18

SEARCH 8
God Accepts Ruth as One of His People

Once, in the time of the judges, there was a *famine*. To find food, Elimelech and his wife, Naomi, left Bethlehem and traveled with their two sons to another land. In this new land Elimelech died. His two sons married, but soon they also died. Then Naomi set out to return to Bethlehem with her daughters-in-law, Orpah and Ruth.

On the road to Bethlehem Naomi told Orpah and Ruth, "Go back to your mother's house." Orpah kissed Naomi good-bye and went back.
CAN YOU FIND ORPAH?

But Ruth stayed. Naomi told her to go back with Orpah. Ruth answered, "No. Wherever you go I will go, your people shall be my people, and your God my God." **CAN YOU FIND NAOMI?**

After they returned to Bethlehem, Ruth went into the fields to gather food. Boaz, who owned the fields, came and greeted his workers. "The Lord be with you," he said. Then he wondered about the girl in the fields. His workers told him that her name was Ruth and she had come to Bethlehem with Naomi.
CAN YOU FIND RUTH?

Boaz was pleased by Ruth's faithfulness to Naomi, so he gathered the city elders at the city gate to get their approval to marry Ruth. The elders agreed to the marriage, so Boaz took Ruth as his wife.
CAN YOU FIND BOAZ?

Ruth and Boaz had a son named Obed, who became the grandfather of King David.

CAN YOU FIND OBED?

SEARCH 9

God Chooses David to Unite the Tribes of Israel

When Samuel, the last great judge, was an old man, the elders of Israel asked him to appoint a king to rule them. Samuel did not want to because he thought God should be the only king of the Israelites. But God said the people could have a king, so Samuel appointed Saul to rule over the Israelites.

God became displeased with Saul so he sent Samuel to Bethlehem to find the man he wanted to replace Saul. In Bethlehem, Samuel found a young man named David, the son of Jesse. Samuel told David that God was with him and that one day he would be king of Israel. **CAN YOU FIND DAVID?**

Some time later, the Philistines sent Goliath, one of their strongest fighters, to frighten the Israelites. David put a stone in his *sling* and threw it toward Goliath. It hit Goliath in the head and killed him. **CAN YOU FIND GOLIATH?**

When Saul died, all the tribes of Israel came to David and agreed to make him King of a united Israel. **CAN YOU FIND KING DAVID?**

After he was King, David had the Ark of the Lord brought to Jerusalem. David danced before the ark as all the Israelites shouted for joy. **CAN YOU FIND THE ARK OF THE LORD?**

Psalm 23
The Divine Shepherd
A Psalm of David

The Lord is my shepherd,
 I shall not want.
He makes me lie down
 in green pastures;
he leads me beside still waters;
 he restores my soul.
He leads me in right paths
 for his name's sake.

Even though I walk through
 the darkest valley,
I fear no evil;
 for you are with me;
your rod and your staff—
 they comfort me.

You prepare a table before me
 in the presence of my enemies;
you anoint my head with oil;
 my cup overflows.
Surely goodness and mercy shall
 follow me all the days of my life,
and I shall dwell in the house of
 the Lord my whole life long.

SEARCH 10
God Allows Solomon to Build a Holy Temple

When David was about to die, he told his son Solomon to do whatever the Lord asked, always walking in his ways and keeping his commands. Then David died and Solomon became king.

In a dream, God told King Solomon to ask for whatever he wanted. Solomon asked to be able to tell the difference between right and wrong. Pleased with Solomon's request, God granted him *wisdom*.
CAN YOU FIND SOLOMON?

Then Solomon built a holy *Temple* for the Lord and put the Ark of the Lord inside it.
Then Solomon prayed to God, thanking him for keeping his covenant of love with Israel.
CAN YOU FIND THE ARK OF THE LORD?

But Solomon was unfaithful to the Lord. He built altars to *pagan* gods on a hill near Jerusalem. This angered the Lord who told Solomon that most of his kingdom would be taken from his son.
CAN YOU FIND THE PAGAN ALTARS?

After being king for forty years, Solomon died. Most of the kings who came after him failed to keep God's commands. Finally, God sent a great prophet named Elijah to warn the Israelites to stop worshiping pagan gods and to turn back to the God of Abraham, Isaac and Jacob.
CAN YOU FIND ELIJAH?

But the Israelites would not listen, so God sent a chariot of fire to bring Elijah safely to heaven. **CAN YOU FIND ELIJAH IN HIS CHARIOT?**

SEARCH 11

God Sends Jonah to Nineveh

To show that he was the God of all the world, God sent a prophet to the pagan city of Nineveh. God picked Jonah and told him to go to the great city of *Nineveh* and tell the people who lived there that they needed to stop being bad or their city would be destroyed.

 But Jonah didn't want to do what God told him to do so he found a ship and sailed away, trying to hide from God. **CAN YOU FIND THE SHIP?**

God sent a storm that almost sank the ship. The other men on the ship asked Jonah what they should do to calm the seas. Jonah, who knew that God was mad at him, told them, "Pick me up and throw me into the sea." So they did. **CAN YOU FIND JONAH?**

God sent a great fish to swallow Jonah and Jonah spent three days and three nights inside the fish. **CAN YOU FIND THE GREAT FISH!**

From inside the fish, Jonah prayed to God saying, "I called to the Lord out of my distress and he answered me." **CAN YOU FIND JONAH PRAYING?**

Then God told the fish to put Jonah on dry land. Again God told Jonah to go to the great city of Nineveh and give the people his message. This time Jonah went to Nineveh and gave the people God's message. All the people, including the king, stopped doing bad things, so God decided not to destroy their city. **CAN YOU FIND NINEVEH?**

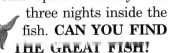

SEARCH 12
God Chooses Esther to Help His People

A few years after the *Babylonian Exile* ended, Babylon was being ruled by a Persian king named Xerxes (ZERK sees). Because his wife, the queen, disobeyed him, Xerxes placed the crown on the head of Esther, a Jewish woman, and made her his queen.

Esther's uncle Mordecai (MORE duh ki) heard of a plot to harm the king. He told Esther who told King Xerxes and so saved the king from harm. **CAN YOU FIND MORDECAI?**

Sometime later, the king realized that he had not done anything to thank Mordecai for saving his life. So Xerxes decided to dress Mordecai in one of his robes, set him on his best horse and parade him through the city. **CAN YOU FIND THE KING?**

A man named Haman was King Xerxes' top official. All the other officials were required to bow down to Haman. Mordecai, who bowed only to the God of Israel, refused to bow. This made Haman so angry he decided to kill Mordecai and all the *Jewish people* in the country. **CAN YOU FIND HAMAN?**

Esther discovered the plan to kill the Jews. She went to King Xerxes and asked him to stop Haman from killing her and her people. **CAN YOU FIND ESTHER?**

King Xerxes agreed to save the Jewish people. He sent messengers by horseback to all corners of his kingdom carrying letters saying that Jewish  people were not to be harmed. **CAN YOU COUNT THE LETTERS?**

SEARCH 13

God Completes His Work of Saving His People

After Adam and Eve ate the fruit God told them not to eat, God made them leave the Garden of Eden. God soon saw that his people would need a lot of help to find their way back to him. The heroes in this book are some of the people God sent to help the Jewish people follow God—to find their way back to the Garden of Eden. God had to send many heroes because his people kept getting in trouble by doing what they wanted to do instead of what God told them to do. But because God loved his people, he always helped them get out of trouble.

God loved his people so much that he eventually sent his Son Jesus to show all people how to follow God. The main message that Jesus brought from his Father was that we should love God as much as he loves us and that we should love our neighbor as much as we love God.

After Jesus returned to heaven, his followers wrote the New Testament to tell us about Jesus. Because Jesus and his followers were Jewish, many of the New Testament stories written about Jesus are connected to Old Testament stories. Reading the Old Testament helps you see these connections and understand Jesus better.

The pairs of searches for this picture, and the stories that go with them, are examples of these connections. The final pair, for the lamps and the star, also show how the Christian feast of Christmas, which welcomes Jesus as the light of the world, is related to Hannukah, the Jewish festival of lights.

In the Old Testament, the lamb's blood that God had the Israelites put over their doors saved them from harm (see Exodus 12:21-23 and Search 5). The Jewish people saw lamb's blood as a symbol of the saving power of God. **CAN YOU FIND THE DOORS?**

At the Last Supper, Jesus shared a cup of wine with his friends. He told them that when he died on the cross his blood would save people from sin (see Matthew 26:27-28). When they heard this, his friends would have thought of the lamb's blood that had saved God's people years before. **CAN YOU FIND THE CUP?**

After God's people left Egypt, they went into the desert. They soon became hungry so God gave them manna to eat (see Exodus 16:2-4 and Search 5). **CAN YOU FIND THE MANNA?**

By the time Jesus finished his Sermon on the Mount, the crowd was hungry. Jesus took five loaves of bread and fed five thousand people. This reminded the people of the long-ago time when God fed the Israelites manna. **CAN YOU FIND THE LOAVES OF BREAD?**

God gave the Ten Commandments to Moses and told him to give these laws to the people (see Exodus 32:15-16 and Search 5). Because of this, Jewish people see Moses as the great lawgiver. **CAN YOU FIND MOSES?**

When Jesus preached the law of God to the Jewish people from a mountainside (see Luke 6:17-49), they would have seen him as another great lawgiver just like Moses. **CAN YOU FIND JESUS?**

After the Jewish people had taken their Temple back from the pagans, the first thing they did was light lamps (see 2 Maccabees 10:1-3) to show that the light of God had come back into the world. **CAN YOU COUNT THE LAMPS?**

After Jesus was born, a special star was seen in the sky (see Matthew 2:1-2). This was a sign, like the lamps, that God's light had come into the world. **CAN YOU FIND THE STAR?**

31

God Creates the World
Genesis 1:3-10, 16-18, 27; 2:15-18; 3

1) After looking over the picture, tell your children that before God created the world there were only God the Father and God the Son, who shared their love through the Holy Spirit. Explain to your children that God understood that love was good and knew he had a lot to share. So God created people, including your children, so he could share his endless love with them. Also explain to your children that God expects us to share this love with those in our lives (parents, grandparents, brothers and sisters, neighbors, teachers). Finally, explain that love is unusual because the more you give away, the more you have left to share.

2) After you find Adam and Eve, discuss with your children what is meant when the Bible says that God created each of us in God's *image*. On almost every page of the Bible there are hints, or clear statements, about the characteristics—the image—of God. Some examples: Matthew 5:1-12: God as teacher and lawgiver; Mark 2:40-42: God as merciful; Luke 8:22-25: God as master of nature; John 6:32: God as life-giver. Explain to your children that when God created us in his image he gave us the ability to reflect these same characteristics—as teachers, as merciful people, as masters of our nature and as givers of life.

3) After finding the angel, read Genesis 3:1-14, the story of Adam and Eve and the fruit of the tree of the knowledge of good and evil. Explain that God made Adam and Eve leave the Garden of Eden because they had become dissatisfied with being God's creatures—with just being an image of God. Point out that by disobeying God and eating the fruit, Adam and Eve were saying to God that they knew more than he did about what was best for people. Finally, point out that when we break God's laws we, like Adam and Eve, are telling God that we think we know better than God how we should live our lives.

4) When you finish the page, explain that after Adam and Eve were sent from the Garden of Eden, people continued to act as if they knew better than God how they should live—they continued to disobey God. As an example, read the Cain and Abel story (Genesis 4:1-16).

5) On a more positive note, point out to your children that the rest of the Bible tells the story of how God has been leading people to special places ever since Adam and Eve were sent out of the Garden of Eden. Please keep this in mind and remind your children of this as you go through the book.

6) Jesus would have been taught that the story of creation was designed to show the power of God. Mary and Joseph would have wanted Jesus to understand the power of God so that it would seem natural for Jesus to join them in the daily praising of the "Lord our God, the Ruler of the Universe." Jesus would also have been taught that the importance of this story, and many of the other stories in the Bible, was not the details themselves, but what the details communicate to us about God and about his relationship with his creation.

God Saves Noah's Family and the Animals
Genesis 6:9, 14-22; 8:8-11; 9:8-13

1) As your children are looking over the page and reading the text, they may wonder why God would flood the world. Remind them that before Noah's time, God had had to send Adam and Eve out of the Garden of Eden because they disobeyed God's command. Now God again looks at the world and sees that people are still disobedient. Also explain that God created and sustains the world and all in it. As Creator, God has given people rules to live by and has the right to hold us accountable when we fail to live as God wants us to. You might try to relate the responsibilities and choices of a parent to God's as the Creator: how parents are responsible for caring for and guiding their children so that they don't get hurt; and disciplining their children when they do things that might harm them. Point out that parents are motivated to guide their children by the same force that motivates God to guide each of us—love.

2) After you have found the ark, talk about Noah's obedience to God—about how Noah stopped what he was doing and did what God asked him to do even though other people made fun of him. Discuss some of the things you and your children do to be obedient to God: go to church, read the Bible, visit the sick, feed the hungry and so on. Next discuss Noah's faith in God's word. There was no sign of a coming flood when Noah started building the ark, but he did so anyway. Explain that this faith in God's word is what makes Noah, and all the characters on the following pages, heroes. Finally, talk about some of the ways you and your children show your faith in God—by praying, by being a good example to all around you, by sharing your possessions with the poor and by sharing your time with the sick and the elderly.

3) When you have finished exploring the page, discuss God's covenant with Noah. Explain that a covenant is an agreement between people to do or not to do certain things. After the flood, because Noah had agreed to build the ark for God, God promised that he would never again flood the world (Genesis 9:8-11). It is important for your children to understand the idea of a covenant because the concept comes up throughout the Bible—there are covenants between God and Abraham, God and Moses, and Jesus and his followers.

4) There are many lessons to be learned from the story of Noah. One Jesus would have been taught is that, although God is just and expects people to obey him, he is also merciful and shows saving mercy to his creation. As a man, Jesus, in faithful obedience to his father, would himself become an example of this lesson by giving his life to save us all from the power of death.

God Calls Abraham to Be the Father of His Chosen People
Genesis 12:6-7; 17:1-19; 18:10-12; 22:1-13

1) After looking over the picture and reading the introductory paragraph, point out that after Adam and Eve left the Garden of Eden they, and the people who came after them, quickly became lost because they did not pay attention to God or look for God's help. Ask your children to try to imagine what would happen to them if they suddenly found themselves in a strange place without you to help them. They would naturally feel lost and afraid. Then explain that you would set out to find your lost children and to help them, just as God set out to help his lost people by talking with Abraham.

2) When you have finished the first search, explain that Abraham and Sarah must have had a lot of faith in God to leave their home and go to a strange land. Remind your children that this faith is the same kind that Noah needed to build the ark. Talk about some of the instances in your life, and in your children's lives, when you show faith in each other: when you trust your children to do their chores, to do their homework, to be polite, to come home on time; when your children trust you to care for them, to pick them up from sports practice, to take them to the doctor when necessary, to love them.

3) After finding Abraham, discuss God's covenant with Abraham with your children. Remind them that a covenant is an agreement between two parties to do certain things. In his covenant with Abraham, God promised Abraham that his descendants would be as numerous as the stars in the sky and promised him he would give these descendants a country to live in (the *promised land*). In return, Abraham agreed to do what God told him to do (see Genesis 15:1-5 and 17:1-9).

4) Jesus must have been deeply moved by the story of Abraham and his beloved son Isaac. He would have been taught that, when God wanted to, he would speak directly to his people—as he had spoken to Abraham. Jesus would have also been taught that because Abraham had faithfully carried out God's instructions, Abraham was considered the Israelites' "Father in Faith." Explain to your children that Abraham is also the Father in Faith for Christians.

God Leads Joseph and the Children of Israel Into Egypt
Genesis 37:12-36; 41:1-49; 42:1-5; 45; 46

1) Read the introductory paragraph, then explain to your children that Jacob, who was now called Israel, had twelve sons. Their names are listed in Genesis 35:23-26. Tell your children that each son was the father of one of the twelve tribes of Israel. Explain that the descendants of Israel's sons came to be called Israelites, and that many of these descendants now live in Israel. Point out that King David, who will be introduced in a later picture, and his descendants came from the tribe of Judah, and that one of David's descendants was Jesus.

2) When you've found the slave Joseph, read Genesis 37:1-4. These verses reveal that Joseph's brothers were jealous of him because their father, Israel, loved Joseph the most of all. If you have more than one child and you feel they are old enough to understand, ask the oldest if she ever feels that you love the younger children more than you love her. If so, explain that often, when a parent appears to love a younger child more than the older ones, it's not a sign that the parent really loves the younger child more, but that the parent has learned from the older children how to show that love better. Also explain that parents sometimes forget that older children (and older people in general—including parents) need to be shown love almost as much as young children do. Discuss additional ways each member of your family can show their love for one other.

3) When you have finished the page, read Genesis 45:4-5 and 50:16-21. In these verses, Joseph assures his brothers that he forgives them for causing him to be taken to Egypt and that what they did worked out for the best; that his going to Egypt put him in a position to save God's Chosen People. Discuss the fact that often we don't know what's best for us. Sometimes we think that not having a certain friend, or not getting to play on that special team, or not getting the new bike we want are the worst things that could happen to us. But we can't really know that. Perhaps the certain friend would have been mean to us, the team would not have been so special, or the new bike might have tempted us to ride dangerously and be hurt. Remind your children that Noah, Abraham and Joseph trusted in God and that each of us should try to do the same.

4) Because Jesus' earthly father was also named Joseph, this was probably a favorite story in Mary and Joseph's home. The Joseph of the story, his eleven brothers and their father Israel were distant relatives of Jesus, so when Jesus listened to this story, he was listening to a story about his own family. One of the lessons Jesus would have been expected to learn from this Bible hero was the importance of forgiveness—that, like Joseph, we should forgive "those who trespass against us." When Jesus became a man he told his followers, including us, many stories that had the same lesson. Review with your children some examples of when you have forgiven each other.

God Chooses Moses
to Lead His People Out of Egypt

Exodus 7—12; 14:10-22; 16:4-15; 31:18; 32:1-6, 15-16;
Deuteronomy 34:1-4

1) Before going over the page, tell your children that, not long after the "Israelites" came to Egypt, as Israel was dying he told his son Joseph, "... God will be with you and will bring you again to the land of your ancestors" (Genesis 48:21). Explain that as the Israelites increased in numbers, the Egyptian rulers started to fear them and so made them into slaves (Exodus 1:8-14). During this period of slavery, which lasted several hundred years, the Israelites persistently called to God to restore them to their "promised" land. Finally God sent Moses to them. Discuss aspects of your child's life in which his persistence has paid off—in schoolwork, in athletics, in music. Point out that persistence is a sign of faith, and that if we persistently pursue a relationship with God, God will respond and lead us to the land he has promised us—heaven, which is the ultimate Garden of Eden.

2) After finding the doors, explain to your children the rules God gave Moses concerning the Passover meal (see Exodus 12:1-17)—particularly the rule that the Israelites were to celebrate this day throughout the generations. Then point out that the meal Jesus shared with his disciples the night before he died—the Last Supper—was also a Passover meal (see Matthew 26:17-19). If your children are able, help them compare the blood of the Passover lamb that saved the Israelites from the plague of death, with the blood of Jesus that saves us from death caused by sin. Explain that this is why Jesus is called "the Lamb of God who takes away the sin of the world" by John the Baptist (see John 1:29).

3) When you have found the clay tablets, tell your children that the Ten Commandments on the tablets are God's laws for us—they are the things God wants us to do or to avoid doing. The Ten Commandments are a clear example of God acting as the great law giver (see Exodus 20:1-17). Point out that God loves us and wants us to be happy, and so gave us laws that, if obeyed, will lead us to happiness. Further explain that the God of the Israelites, the God of Abraham, Isaac and Jacob, is also our God. For this reason, Jesus tells us that we must continue to obey the laws given the Israelites by Moses and the other *prophets* (Matthew 5:17-20). By obeying God's laws, we will be showing God that we love him and know he loves us.

4) As in the story of Abraham, one of the lessons Jesus would have been taught about Moses is that God can and does speak directly to his people. Jesus would also have been told that he, and all God's people, owed God unending gratitude for having freed them from slavery in Egypt, and that in freeing his people from slavery God had "redeemed" them. Finally, Jesus' parents and teachers would have painted a picture of God as the great lawgiver, who called Moses to the mountain to be given the law, which Moses then took to God's people. Jesus, during his ministry, presented himself as the great lawgiver when he gave the Sermon on the Mount (see Matthew 5—7). The Jews to whom Jesus was speaking would have been reminded of Moses as they listened to Jesus explain God's laws.

God Appoints Joshua
to Lead the Israelites

Deuteronomy 31:14-15, 23;
Joshua 2:1-7, 15-21; 6:1-5, 12, 20-23

1) After looking at the spread, discuss Joshua's faith in the Lord with your children. Read Joshua 1:1-11. In these verses God tells Joshua to be strong and faithful, and then promises Joshua that if he is *faithful*, God will bring the Israelites safely to the promised land. Remind your children that it is Joshua's willingness to do what God wants him to do that makes him, and the rest of the men and women in this book, heroes.

2) When you've found the ark, tell your children that the ark was a wooden box God had Moses build to carry the stone tablets on which the ten commandments were written (Exodus 39:32-43). Explain that it was a symbol to the Israelites that God was accompanying his people. Tell your children that soon after the Israelites entered the promised land, God stopped sending the manna to feed them (Joshua 5:10-12). Now that God had fulfilled his promise and brought his people to the land of "milk and honey," he expected them to start taking care of themselves. Explain that although God loves us unceasingly, at some point God expects us, with divine help and the help of grace, to participate actively in providing for ourselves. Connect this relationship with God to your relationship with your children. Your love for your children leads you to take care of them—to feed, clothe, shelter and watch over them. But at some point you expect your children to begin to provide for themselves. Make clear that you consider this independence to be a sign that your love has succeeded in helping your children become the mature adults God wishes them to be. Finally point out that this maturity in your children is a reason to love them even more.

3) After finding Joshua, remind your children that each of the heroes in this book was sent by God to help us on our journey back to God, and that this journey through the Old Testament leads us to Jesus, who shows us how to complete our journey from sin to knowing and loving God.

4) Mary and Joseph and the other teachers in Jesus' life would probably have wanted Jesus to focus on Joshua's faith in the word of God. Most people would have laughed at the idea that marching around a city blowing horns would knock down strong stone walls. But Joshua believed that whatever God told him to do was the best thing he could do. Explain to your children that when Jesus became a teacher he taught us that fighting to get what you want was no longer pleasing to God (see Matthew 5:38-48, Matthew 7:12, Matthew 26:51-52, Mark 8:34-38, Luke 6:27 and John 15:12-13).

God Picks Judges
to Help His Chosen People
Judges 4:4-16; 7:9-22; 16:23-30;
1 Samuel 4:12-18; 5-7:4

1) After looking over the picture, point out that the period covered by this page was one in which God's people, the Israelites, often were disobedient (see Judges 2:13-19 and 6:7-10). Explain that each time God's people disobeyed God, they got into trouble, as children might do when they disobey their parents. Next explain that, like a good parent, God helped those children in need. The help took the form of various men and women who were called judges. Finally, point out that the men and women called judges on this page weren't judges in the modern sense—they didn't sit in a courtroom. They were leaders, often military heroes, who did what God told them to do to get God's people out of the trouble they had gotten themselves into.

2) When you've found Samson, explain that the temple he destroyed was one for the pagan god Dagon. Read Judges 6:25-28, where the judge Gideon destroys an altar to the pagan god Baal. Explain that one of the major reasons the Israelites kept getting into trouble was they would abandon the God of Abraham, Isaac and Jacob (who is also our God) and start to *worship* false gods. Point out that in the modern world persons and things can become "false gods"—persons or things that take the place of God in our lives. Ask your children for some examples of modern false gods—rock bands, movie actors, athletes, tennis shoes or jackets, fancy cars, big houses, high-paying jobs. Make sure your children understand that rock stars and high-paying jobs aren't bad in themselves, but only become bad when we let them push God out of our lives.

3) After you have located Eli, explain that it was Eli's parental duty to tell his sons that their disrespect for God would eventually get them into trouble. Explain to your children that each of us is responsible for trying our best, whether at schoolwork, sports, parenting or obeying God. Help them understand that we may not succeed all the time, but that we can't let the fear of failing scare us into not trying to do our best.

4) The teachers of Jesus would have emphasized the faithfulness of God to his people as shown by his sending the judges to help them. God's faithfulness to his people is one of the ongoing themes of Jewish history. Faith that God would help his people when they called on him has been one of the identifying characteristics of the Jewish people since the time of Moses. When Jesus became a teacher he often spoke of God's faithfulness to those who trust in him (see Matthew 8:13, Matthew 9:27-29, Mark 10:51-52, Luke 5:17-20, Luke 18:6-8, John 11:32-44).

God Accepts Ruth
as One of His People
Ruth 1:7-18; 2:1-8; 4:1-11, 13-22

1) After finding Naomi, explain that the Israelites took their responsibility as the chosen people of God very seriously. Part of this responsibility that God had given them was to introduce the one true God—the God of Abraham, Isaac and Jacob—to the rest of the people in the world. For this reason Naomi's family would have happily accepted Ruth into the family of faith in the one true God. Point out that it was Ruth's faithfulness to Naomi and to Naomi's God that impressed Naomi's relatives, especially Boaz (see Ruth 2:10-13). Explain that it was this faithfulness that inspired Boaz to marry Ruth and provide her with a happy home and family.

2) When you have found Ruth, point out to your children that some grain was left in the fields for the poor to gather for their food. Leviticus 23:22 reads, "When you reap the harvest of your land, you shall not reap to the very edges of your field or gather the gleanings [stray ears] of your harvest. You shall leave them for the poor and the alien [stranger]. I, the Lord, am your God." These are pretty clear instructions from the Lord—it's almost as if he is telling his Chosen People to invite the poor and the stranger into their fields by leaving a little food in them. It is certainly clear that the Lord wants his people to provide for the poor and the stranger. Point out some ways that God's people respond to this call today: by donating food and money to their church; by working at food banks or soup kitchens; by praying for the poor; by paying taxes, some of which is used to help the poor and the stranger; by providing clothes and blankets to the local homeless shelter, and so on. Discuss together how you can participate in some of these modern ways of not gathering the stray ears.

3) The teachers of Jesus would have emphasized Ruth's willingness, as a non-Jew (a stranger), to join the Jewish people. Most of the pagan peoples in the countries surrounding the Jewish nation considered the God of Israel to be a stern God. He demanded a lot from his people: faithfulness, obedience and love of both God and neighbor. These were demands that not many pagans were willing to respond to. Yet these are the requirements that were placed upon Ruth and Jesus and his friends when they were children, and are demands that Jesus emphasized in his ministry.

God Chooses David
to Unite the Tribes of Israel
1 Samuel 16:1-13; 17:20-51; 2 Samuel 5:1-3; 6:11-15

1) After finding David, tell your children that God became displeased with Saul because Saul disobeyed him. This is why God sent Samuel to Bethlehem to find the son of Obed, Jesse, who had many sons. Samuel first saw one of Jesse's older and more impressive-looking sons and thought he must be the one God had chosen. But God told Samuel, "Do not look on his appearance, because I have rejected him; for the Lord does not see as mortals [people] see; they look on the outward appearance, but the Lord looks on the heart" (see 1 Samuel 16:1-13). Point out to your children that God is not saying we should ignore a person's appearance, but that we need to look deeper than that and try to see as God sees. This is what Mother Teresa tried to do. When she reached out to pick up a sick and dying child she saw that the child was diseased and perhaps dirty, but she also looked into the heart of the child and saw a reflection of God—the child's soul.

2) After finding the Ark of the Lord, look for musical instruments around the tent. Tell your children that David and the rest of God's people often used music and song to praise God. David himself was a skilled and famous harpist (see 1 Samuel 16:14-18). The Book of Psalms contains many of the songs that the Jewish people used, and still use, to ask for God's help, to praise God and to thank him for all he has done and continues to do for his creation. Point out that many of the psalms are prefaced by the name of the writer (David wrote some of them) and even the instruments that should be used to accompany the singing are sometimes listed. Finally explain that this is why we have music in our churches—so that we can join with the choirs of angels and saints in praising God.

3) When you have finished the page, read 2 Samuel 7:8-16. Explain that in Nathan's prophecy God promised David that one of his descendants would be a son to God and that his kingdom would last forever. Point out that Jesus was born in Bethlehem (the city of David) because his father Joseph was of the "house and family of David" (see Luke 2:1-5). This is one of the many prophecies concerning the Messiah that Christians believe were fulfilled by Jesus (see Zechariah 9:9 and Isaiah 7:14).

4) Jesus would have seen David as the great uniter of the tribes of Israel. For the first time, under David's kingship, Israel had a single earthly ruler. Jesus would also have been taught that David was important because he captured Jerusalem and made it the capital of the country.

God Allows Solomon
to Build a Holy Temple
1 Kings 3:5-15; 8:3-23; 11-18; 2 Kings 2:9-11

1) After finding Solomon, explain to your children that wisdom is understanding that right actions are those that please God and wrong actions are those that displease God. Remind the children that God gave them (and continues to give them) life because he loves them. This is the reason we should want to be wise and to do what is right—because God loves us. Describe how parents and grandparents try to do what is right for the children in their lives for the same reason—because they love them. Finally, describe a series of actions to the children and ask them to tell you if the action is right or wrong. If the children are able, ask them to explain to you why they think the action is right or wrong. Try to help them focus on the idea that wrong actions displease God. For example, if a child says that hitting someone is wrong, point out that what makes it wrong is that the person you hit is loved by God and therefore hurting the person hurts God.

2) When you have found the Temple, tell your children that after it was built God warned Solomon never to worship any other god (see 1 Kings 9:4-9). But over the years Solomon allowed many people from the pagan lands that surrounded Jerusalem to come and live in his palace (see 1 Kings 11:1-13). Eventually it became too much trouble for Solomon to "walk in the ways of the Lord," as David had told him he must do. These pagans turned Solomon's heart away from the Lord and he worshiped some of the pagan gods. Explain that Solomon, and most of the kings who came after him, forgot that to be a king for God you have to first become God's servant by always "walking in his ways" (John 13:12-16). Give your children examples of some of the ways your family walks in the ways of God.

3) After you finish the page, explain that Elijah was the first of a series of great prophets. Remind your children that a prophet is somebody who has a message from God to give to other people. Isaiah came soon after Elijah and warned God's people that they had forgotten the Lord and become a sinful people (see Isaiah 1:1-4). Jeremiah came next with the message that God's people had turned away from the Lord and were not returning to him (see Jeremiah 5). Jeremiah also told God's people that God would abandon them because they had abandoned him (see Jeremiah 21:1-10). After God abandoned them, the people of Israel were conquered by their pagan neighbors. Then God sent another prophet, Ezekiel, to tell his people that he would one day restore them to the promised land (see Ezekiel 36:20-38). This restoration took place as described in Ezra 1:1-8.

4) Jesus would have been taught that Solomon was the great King who had built the Holy Temple as a place for God to be present with his people. The Temple was so important to the young Jesus that he spent three days there—in his father's house (see Luke 2:41-52)—discussing God's law with the teachers. Later in life, Jesus drove the merchants from the Temple (see Mark 11:15-17) because they had turned his father's house from a holy place into a marketplace and had forgotten that the Temple was a place to praise God.

God Sends Jonah to Nineveh
Jonah 1:1-15, 17; 2:2, 10; 3:1-10

1) After looking over the spread, tell your children that Nineveh was a city in a country near where the Israelites lived that had often waged war against God's chosen people. Explain that God's prophets usually spoke only to God's chosen people, but that this time God was telling his prophet to go to a foreign country to tell its people that the God of Israel says they must repent of their evil ways. Point out that, in the same way, Jesus would reach out to all the peoples of the world and proclaim that the God of Abraham, Isaac and Jacob was the God of all humanity. See Matthew 12:38-42.

2) When you have found the ship, explain to your children that Jonah was a "reluctant" prophet. When God first told him to go to Nineveh, Jonah ran away. Then, because he refused to do what God wanted him to do, Jonah ended up being thrown into the sea. But God saved him and gave him another chance and this time Jonah did what God wanted him to do. Point out that, as a parent, you give your children second (and third) chances—give some examples such as washing dishes, cleaning rooms and doing homework. Tell your children that, as with Jonah, God also gives us second chances. While God would like us to do what he wants the first time he asks us, he will ask us again and again (to obey our parents, to love our family and neighbors, to praise him, to be honest) until we, like Jonah, finally obey.

3) After finding the great fish, ask your children if they think a person could really spend three days and three nights inside a big fish. With very young children the answer may be yes. Older children will be more realistic and answer no. Point out to them that one of the points of this story is that God, who created the world out of nothing, can do anything he wants. Explain that nature, and all that is in it, came from God (see Search 1: God Creates the World) and that God can use or change nature in any way he wants to. Remind your children of the New Testament stories in which Jesus cures the sick, walks on water, is transfigured and rises from the dead.

4) When you have finished the spread, point out that God forgave the pagan people who lived in Nineveh, just as he had often forgiven his chosen people. Ask your children if they think this example of forgiveness is one God wants each of us to follow. Remind them of the Lord's Prayer, the Sermon on the Mount (Matthew 5) and the story of the merciless official (Matthew 18: 21-35).

5) While Jesus and his young friends probably would not have thought too much about whether Jonah actually spent three days inside a fish, they would have been taught a lot about what this story told them about God's relationship with his creation. First, they would have been taught that the story of Jonah shows that you can't run from God, for he will track you down wherever you try to hide. They would also have been taught that Jonah's being sent to the pagans in Nineveh showed that the God of Abraham, Isaac and Jacob wanted to be the God of all the world. Jesus and his friends would certainly have been taught that, as sons and daughters of Israel, they were responsible for helping bring the one true God (of Abraham, Isaac and Jacob) to their pagan neighbors. As a man, Jesus would tell his disciples to spread the good news of the Gospel to the ends of the earth (see Matthew 28:18-20).

God Chooses Esther to Help His People
Esther 2:21-22; 3:1-7; 6:1-11; 7:1-4; 8:9-11

1) After looking over the page, remind your children that about one hundred years before this story took place the Jewish people had been driven out of Jerusalem and scattered throughout the Persian Empire. This was the beginning of the Diaspora: the scattering of the Jewish people throughout the world. Also explain that about fifty years before Esther, the Jews had been allowed to return to Jerusalem. Many had done so, but many stayed in scattered towns and cities where they had started new lives.

2) When you have found Haman, explain that Haman, by forcing the rest of the King's officials to bow down before him, was being set up as someone to be worshiped—as a god. The Ten Commandments of Mordecai's God forbade him to worship false gods (see Exodus 20:1-6 and Deuteronomy 6:10-15). Discuss with your children the false gods that might tempt them in their lives: money, pride, power and any others you feel are appropriate. Explain that in the end, these false gods will desert us, and that unless we hold on to the one true God, like Mordecai did, we will end up with nothing.

3) After counting the letters, read Esther 9:20-23. These verses explain the origin of the Jewish feast of Purim. Mordecai instructed the Jewish people to celebrate forever the anniversary of their being saved from Haman's plan to wipe them out. This celebration is the feast of Purim. Each year Jewish children dress up and act out the story of how Esther and Mordecai, guided by God, saved the Jewish people from physical destruction. Compare this playacting to that done by Christian children during Christmas pageants.

4) Jesus, who lived some four hundred years after the story of Esther took place, would have been taught that this story was another example of God stepping in and saving his people. Jesus would have celebrated the feast of Purim, perhaps even dressing up and taking part in the reenactment of the story. Later in life, Jesus would offer his life to save us from spiritual destruction.

God Completes His Work
of Saving His People

1) After looking over the page, explain to your children that because Jesus was Jewish and was speaking mostly to other Jewish people, he often explained things using examples from the Old Testament—examples with which his audiences were very familiar. Also explain that because the people who wrote the New Testament were Jewish, they often used stories or quotes from the Old Testament when writing about Jesus to make it easier for those who read or heard the New Testament to understand Jesus.

2) When you have found the doors and the cup, tell your children that on the first Passover it was the blood of the lamb that saved the lives of the Israelites—the Chosen People of God. Through the years, as the Israelites continued to celebrate Passover (see Exodus 12:14-17), the lamb came to be looked upon as a symbol of salvation and God came to be looked on as the "redeemer." Read John 1:29, in which John the Baptist calls Jesus "...the Lamb of God who takes away the sin of the world." Explain that by calling Jesus "the Lamb of God," John was saying that, in some way, Jesus would provide further redemption. Explain that at the Last Supper Jesus was saying to his Apostles that his blood, which would be shed on the cross, would bring that further redemption.

3) After finding the manna and the loaves of bread, remind your children that in both instances God gave his people bread because in the times of Moses and Jesus bread was the most important food. God gave his people bread because he wanted them to see that he was the source and sustainer of their lives. Jesus called himself "...the bread of life" for the same reason (see John 6:25-51).

4) After locating Moses and Jesus, explain that Jesus taught the law of God from a mountainside (see Matthew 5:1-2) because he wanted the people to see him as a great lawgiver like Moses, who came down the mountain with God's laws on stone tablets. Because Jesus' audience already understood the story of Moses as lawgiver, Jesus wanted to use this understanding to help the crowd understand that he, too, was a lawgiver.

5) When you have found the lamps and the star, explain that artificial light, like that from a lamp, was very important in Biblical times. Most of the time, after the sun set, people were in the dark, where it was easy to stumble and fall or get lost. The lamps in the Temple, and in many modern churches, are there to remind us that God is the true light of the world and that if we are close to God we will not get lost in the dark (see John 8:12). Explain that when the lamps in the Temple were relit, this symbolized the light of God returning to his people. This event is remembered by the Jewish people during the winter festival of Hannukah, which begins on the 25th of the Jewish month of Chislev, when lights are lit and children are given presents. Then explain that when Jesus was born a great light appeared in the sky to show that Jesus was to be the "light of the world". Jesus' birth is remembered by Christians during the winter festival of Christmas, on the 25th of our winter month of December.

Glossary

Altar A raised platform where offerings are made to God.

Angel A messenger from God.

Ark A large boat.

Ark of the Lord A wooden box in which the Israelites carried the tablets with the ten commandments written on them.

Babylonian Exile A period of around one hundred years when the Jewish people were forced to leave their own country and live in foreign cities.

Bless To set apart for a holy purpose; to make happy.

Camp A place where men and equipment were gathered together to prepare for battle.

Canaan The land north of Egypt into which God led Abraham and his family.

Commandment An order to do or not to do something.

Covenant An agreement between two people, or a people and their God, to do or not to do certain things.

Create To make something out of nothing.

Descendants All the people in your family who come after you.

Disobey To refuse to do what you are told to do.

Evil Bad and wicked; disobedient to God.

Faith A belief in something based on trust in God and confidence in God's word.

Faithful Being strong in what you believe and living it out.

Famine A time when plants do not grow well and there is little food for people to eat.

Holy Spirit The active presence of God in our life; God's love shared with us.

Image A person who looks and acts the same as another person.

Jewish people Any of the descendants of God's chosen people—also called Hebrews or Israelites.

Locusts Insects that are like grasshoppers, which eat plants. A swarm of locusts can eat all of the plants and crops in a large area.

Lord Someone who has great power. God is often called "the Lord."

Manna Small flakes of bread that God sent to feed the Israelites in the desert.

Midianites Members of a wandering tribe of Arabs who came from Midian.

Nineveh A city in ancient Assyria, on the Tigris River, about 600 miles from Jerusalem.

Pagan As used by the Israelites, a pagan was anyone who did not follow the God of Abraham.

Pharaoh The title for the kings of ancient Egypt.

Philistines People who lived near the Israelites and often battled with them for control of the land.

Plague Widespread disease or a large number of pests like locusts or frogs.

Priest A person who makes sacrifices for the people and performs other religious ceremonies.

Promised land The land of Canaan that God promised to give to the descendants of Abraham (see Genesis 17:1-9, Deuteronomy 32:48-49 and Joshua 1:1-3).

Prophet/Prophetess A person who speaks for God.

Sacrifice To present something to God as a sign of a person's dedication to God. The Israelites sacrificed animals to God, Jesus sacrificed his life for us, and today we sacrifice time, or food (through fasting), or perhaps some material possessions to share with the poor.

Slave A person who has lost his or her freedom and is owned by another person.

Sling A strap that is used to throw stones.

Spies Persons who sneak into another country to see what is going on.

Tablets Stone slabs that have writing on them.

Temple A place set aside for a god to live in. The Temple in Jerusalem was the place where the God of Israel was present among his people in a special way.

Wisdom The ability to make the best use of knowledge of both God and God's world.

Worship To respect, honor and adore.